Good Parenting:

5 tips on how to be the best parents for your children

Rachel M. Gosseli

Dedication

My family motivated and inspired me to write this book, thus it is dedicated to them.

TABLE OF CONTENTS

INTRODUCTION

Parents are among the most crucial persons in the lives of young children, from birth children are learning and rely on mothers and dads, as well as other caregivers acting in the parenting role, to secure and care for them and to build a trajectory that promotes their overall well-being.

While parents are generally excited with anticipation about their children's growing personalities, many frequently lack knowledge on how best to care for them. Becoming a parent is typically a joyous affair, but in rare cases, parents' lives are fraught with obstacles and anxiety about their ability to sustain their child's physical, mental, or economic well-being.

To ensure pleasant experiences for their children, parents depend on the resources of which they are aware or that are at their immediate disposal.

In this book, Good parenting it helps promote empathy, honesty, self-reliance, self-control, compassion, teamwork, and happiness. It also enhances intellectual curiosity and motivation and creates a will to succeed.

Chapter 1

Love your kids

We must not love out of selfishness and fear, you want to do your best to raise your kid as such, it's reasonable to worry that you show them too much attention or give them too much love without adequate discipline.

You don't want to tolerate and encourage undesirable behaviors, but you should not fall into the trap of "letting them weep" or "letting them tough it out," leaving your child feeling like a very little person alone in a very large world.

Experts today believe that the idea of tough love is a failed parenting strategy, your child has to create a good link with you to avoid behavioral issues and difficulties in their future relationships.

There's no such thing as delivering too much love to your kids regrettably, your children won't gain this lesson in school or society at large. That leaves you teaching that love comes first may be as enjoyable as playing football for a day of unstructured play instead of following the usual work-school cycle.

Too much discipline, from homework to soccer practice to Bible study, leaves your kids hungry for outlets for their innate creativity.

Teaching your kids that there is no such thing as too much love helps them develop emotional intelligence,

Embracing the concept that there's no such thing as delivering too much love to your child helps them create a secure bond.

Psychologists have identified four fundamental attachment types—one safe and three insecure.
Those who fall within the insecure category often experience future challenges in partnerships.

There are four main attachment types

1. Anxious

Also described as obsessive, these individuals tend to become excessively controlling in relationships, sometimes grasping so tightly that they push the other person away.

2. Avoidant

Also labeled as dismissive, these persons usually push others away purposefully, adopting the mindset that they are ruggedly independent.
They could struggle to build bonds and express affection.

3. Disorganized

Also known as fearful-avoidant, this style shows persons who yearn to be close but, paradoxically, flee from relationships.

They may go through a hot-and-cold cycle, feeling someone is their soulmate one day and their greatest enemy the next.

4. Secure

People with this attachment type form good connections with mutual respect and fair limitations.

Your child's attachment type develops during their early years based on their relationship with you.

Facts for Fostering Secure Attachment

If you didn't have the finest upbringing, you might struggle with how to offer your children, unconditional love.
That's alright-accepting the following recommendations will help you master safe attachment parenting.

1. Give Time and Presence as Gifts.

There's no replacement for your time and presence in your kid's life they may understand the odd rush period at work, but putting in more hours all the time at the expense of your relationship can impact your child in the long term.

It could make them adopt an avoidant style, believing they must take care of things alone because they can’t count on you for encouragement and support.

Make a fuss for their birthday, you don’t need the means to organize a gala, but you should spend the day together. Schedule at least one activity weekly where you share something you like, whether it's digging in the yard or racing around the playground.

2. When correcting conduct, encourage love.

You may still chastise your child’s disobedience while showering them with affection the key is to remove the transgression from the kids.

You may do so by emphasizing how much you adore them while you repair them.
Say something like, "I love you very much, but when you keep yelling while I have a headache, I feel annoyed and wounded." You teach a dual lesson in identifying feelings and addressing misbehavior while letting your child maintain their essential dignity.

3. Validate Your Child's Feelings

Your kid isn't born knowing how to label their feelings — or whether their emotions are acceptable to the environment, all they know is that they have "big feelings" that make them act out in interesting ways.
Part of offering your child love includes acknowledging their feelings, instead of

answering, the "Don't weep," question, "What's wrong?"

Help them clarify their experience, are they weeping out of frustration or fear?

Let them know it's okay to feel the way they do. What is essential is how they handle their emotions.

Help them explore strategies to comfort themselves properly so they can handle stress later in life.

4. Genuinely Recognize Achievements

Your kids badly needs your approval to give them affection by expressing real praise for their efforts. Maybe that finger painting isn't the greatest you've ever seen but it is certainly the most colorful and inventive.

Offering genuine appreciation for your child's successes helps them improve their self-esteem. It also instills agency—the sense that their actions can positively influence their reality.

Chapter 2

Spending quality time with your children

As the days go by, our activities lists become greater and other commitments tend to take precedence over vital family time.
Study reveals that it is vital to schedule recurring family time with your children.
As busy parents, you spend ample time with your children, but it is genuine quality time.

Quality time spent with your children and giving them your undivided attention while accomplishing duties that they like.
Spending quality time with your children does not have to be a major chore. It may be

as basic as spending a few minutes each day together without any interruptions.
So why is quality time with our kids so important?

So, kids are less likely to develop behavioral difficulties at home or school, and children who are spending more quality time with their families are less likely to participate in dangerous activities such as drug misuse.

Showing your children that you love and care for them helps to maintain them mentally and emotionally resilient.
As a parent, the ideal method to do this is to spend quality time with them daily.
Children who spend more quality time with their families are more likely to be physically healthy.

Overall, spending quality time with your children is critical to them but is also important to your well-being.

Here are some simple ideas for spending quality time with your children:

1. Connect every day with your kids.

Whether it be face-to-face encounters before school and work or putting them a quick note in their lunch bags, any type of connection with your children is vital and valuable. Tell your child that you love them every day, Let your kidss know why you love and adore them. Create some usual routine, such as picking and reading a short book before night.
Reinforce positive conduct with your praise.

2. Cook supper and eat together.

This helps the family to speak with one another as well as establish a partnership. Schedule time to do an activity with your child; let them select. such as handicrafts, baking, family game night, etc. Even if it is just for a few minutes, try to play with your toddler.

Tell jokes and giggle with your kiddies. Laughter is vital for boosting emotional well-being.

Take a half-hour vacation from gadgets and spend time listening to and speaking with your kids.

Making a true connection with your children is vital and maybe a simple objective to incorporate 'into your everyday routine.

Doing so will have enduring repercussions for children as they grow into productive persons in the future.

Are you spending enough quality time with your children?

Life is stressful, and we know that this is especially true for parents and families. Our responsibilities at hand get larger, and we have other priorities that take priority over valuable family time, some days we are so busy caring for our children's needs that we rarely have time for a break.

We have so much on our hands to take care of cooking, washing dishes, laundry, clothes, reprimanding harsh behavior, and so many other things.

When you feel like your entire day revolves around your children, it seems foolish to even think about this issue.

What else am I doing if not spending time with them?

Quality time entails giving them your complete attention and doing what they like doing.

It may be as basic as taking a few minutes every day with no other distractions in place.

You are proving to your children that you love and care for them, which will benefit their cognitive and emotional growth.

We will be looking at the ways of spending time with your children and the benefits of it, as Sherwood High fully believes in the significance of spending time with your children.

3. Schedule a certain time for your child.

Connect with your kids every day, whether it's before school or after, during break times, or before sleep, and set aside specific time for activities with your child.

This may also be a family fun time when you and your spouse may make use of this time together with the kids, or you can take turns with your children according to your free schedules.

Avoiding distractions: When spending time with your kid, keep away from any electronics, switch off your gadgets, and avoid performing any housework or office work.

Avoid sending or receiving texts and calls during this time, and avoid TV ad music unless it is part of the task that you are doing.

Allow your kid to pick what to do, whether they want to ride a bike, play with their toys, bake a cake, or performing arts and crafts, let them decide what makes them happy and be part of that activity.
Spend a lot of time laughing together.
Tell a lot of jokes and laugh with your kids, as laughing helps strengthen both physical and mental health.

Parent as a friend: This comes into play when dealing with teenagers.
As the dynamics of the relationship become complex, you need to comprehend them

from their point of view, and what they are going through.
At this stage, you need to treat your baby like a friend to win their trust, no matter how hard it looks.

The ideal approach to connect with them would be to know when to come in as a parent and when to be a friend.

You need to interact with them and share your experiences regarding the concerns and difficulties you faced growing up, the mistakes you made, and how you sought to remedy your shortcomings.

This will help your teenager respect you and be honest, which will in turn boost the bonding process.

Two important Benefits of Spending Time with Your Children:

1. Helps improve children's self-esteem: Children whose parents take part in activities together acquire a high sense of self-worth.

kids think that their parents admire them, and this improves optimism and self-esteem.

Nurturing a caring environment: When there is love and harmony between the parents and the children, the effect reverberates about you and offers a loving, reliable, and pleasant atmosphere that assists in fostering excellent conduct and academic success.

Kids who spend more time with their parents to get involved in risky behavior, also spending time with them with their schoolwork or doing activities like reading to them or reading with them, will foster an environment where your children will value education and will be more likely to perform better academically.

2. Decreasing stress: Being a parent is tough, Balancing between work, personal interests, parenting, and other responsibilities may be demanding, and spending time with your kids may operate as a stress buster because spending time with your children helps you relax and brings out the best in you.

It assists in building communication skills. When you are spending time with your children, you're also building an atmosphere that is open for conversation.

Strong communication is vital for your children to feel comfortable with what they talk about.

Just by asking your kid how their day was, you may have a tremendous impact on their communication abilities.

Strengthens Family Bonds: Families that spend time often and share day-to-day activities establish strong emotional bonds.

Chapter 3

Teach Your Child how to be Independent.

Children are too young to comprehend the notion of timeliness or to accept responsibility for their conduct unless they are taught the same by their parents.

Your young one can be dependent on you for minor things, and he may require you for basic things until you allow him the freedom to do things on his own, make errors, and learn from them.

As your child develops, you will want to make him autonomous, and appropriate since your basic orders should not come as a punishment.

As a parent, you may guide your kids on the correct path with a few simple pieces of advice and allow your child to explore freedom in his manner.

Why Should Kids Learn to Be Independent?

Your child might be too little right now, but ultimately, he will grow up to be a fully functioning adult.

Learning a few basic skills early in childhood can equip him to meet the rigors of maturity.

Children take a time to learn the notion of options and make a decision that they think is best for them. By introducing options

early on in their lives, children may start understanding themselves better and realize what makes them happy.
Life isn't all bliss and satisfaction all around. There will be occasions when your child can fail to perform what was required of him.
But if he is autonomous, he will identify his faults, come to you for assistance, and be open to advice on doing better.

Self-esteem within a person is established at such an early age. And this can be greater if a kids starts having trust in himself and his judgments. Independence helps in this area and lets a kids feel valued early on.

Books contain information but wisdom is obtained only through deeds. The gap between warning your kids about the danger and your small one encountering it is a tremendous one. Being independent helps your child to start learning things by himself, take chances, and be more educated as a person.

How to Teach Your Child to Be Independent

There are several methods to raise your child to be independent and yet enjoy his childhood the way he deserves.

1. Give Him Responsibilities He Can Handle

Your kids does not need to start controlling the economics of the house and make important decisions. Independence needs to originate with the self and that is where you can aid your child.

If you are preparing a picnic and need your child to help you out with it, offer him easy chores such as drafting a list of products you might need or going ahead and packing his suitcase for a short weekend trip you could be on.

2. Avoid Hand-Holding Your Child.

Many parents confuse guiding with hand-holding and continuously intervene in the child's behavior if he is doing something incorrectly or is taking longer than needed. When your child is young, it is helpful to lead your child with some directions or open-ended ideas that notify him of the possibility that the work might be accomplished in an easier method. But as he grows older, let him come to you if he needs help, rather than meddling needlessly.

3. Introduce Choices With Limited Options

Asking your child what he would like to eat at a restaurant might get very daunting for him as the restaurant menu is quite broad. Instead, choose a variety of items from the menu and ask him to choose from the selected possibilities. Starting with a restricted array can help him make a choice simply and prepare him for newer ones.

4. Let Your Child Make His Own Decisions At Times

You could want to make your kids finish his schoolwork before he goes out to play. But he could prefer playing first to doing his homework. Allow your child some degree of choice in minor things, such as deciding what to dress or what snack to eat in the evening. And as long as he accomplishes what he promises, you shouldn't have an issue.

5. Have Empathy Towards Your Child.

Your kids is only starting to be independent, therefore it won't be easy for him. Avoid criticizing him or putting him down, especially if he fails to perform something relatively basic. Be there to encourage him and assist him out if he asks for it, without criticizing him.

6. Don't Make Failures a Big Issue.

There may be instances when your child might fail at something, and certainly, he will be unhappy. Comfort him and let him know that it's acceptable to fail.

Teach him to learn from those failures, get up and try again. He could even repeat them despite your cautions. It's okay, let him learn from his errors.

Do let your child know what he might have done better, but don't associate the failure with him. This might affect his self-esteem iimmensely.

7. Teach Your Child to Solve Problems Independently

Be it school-related troubles or any issues he might have with siblings or friends, let your child know that certain problems have to be managed by him and you can't help him with those. Guide him if required by offering him an alternative view on the mamatter.

8. Establish a Proper Routine

Children might have problems making judgments for themselves if they don't think sequentially. This may be readily managed by defining a consistent procedure for them. Once your kids learns what has to be done on a given day and at a specific time, he will start doing it all by himself.

9. Teach Negotiation

Many kidss tend to start perceiving the world as a win-and-loss scenario. Open up your kids to the realm of compromise and bargaining and he will start understanding to make the best of the scenario that is put before him.

He can either select the picnic site or the picnic meal but he cannot do both. This will help him prioritize his own choices, too.

There's quite a distinction between making toddlers autonomous and training them to complete specific things by themselves. But as your child becomes adjusted to the surroundings at school, you may ask him to undertake the simple exercises by himself. These might steadily cultivate the seeds of independence in him.

Chapter 4

Give a listening ear to your kids and get them to actually listen to you.

As a parent, it may be incredibly irritating when your kid looks like he or she is not listening, or worse still, seems to actively disregard you.

You may worry about what you're doing wrong or whether your kids is unusually defiant.

But the reality is that there are a variety of reasons why kids don't listen, including that they simply haven't learned this capacity yet.

Regardless of the issues you're having when it comes to your child's listening abilities, it helps to grasp a few of the reasons for their failure to listen.

It's also good to have a few tactics up your sleeve that can help you cultivate better listening skills in your kids.

What to Do When Your Child Ignores Directions? Why Children Don't Listen

Getting a reluctant kids to listen may be difficult at times for parents.

It's typical to see listening habits in terms of respect: "If my kid won't listen and pay attention, but rather appears preoccupied all the time, it is a sign of contempt."

Truth be told, failing to listen is not always about respect.

It's also a stage kids go through as they strive to sort out their reality, so although it may seem like disrespect, it's usually about something far more fundamental.

Sometimes kids struggle to listen because your messages are too lengthy or you're coming across as critical or whining.

But more often than not, failing to listen well is more about your child's social development than anything else.

As early as the infant years, some toddlers may purposely misbehave to see how parents and caregivers respond.

Even though you understand Even though you understand that a child's incapacity to listen is most likely developmental, it nevertheless may be worrisome when you feel that playing, the television, or video games are more important than what you have to say.

When it comes to educating kidss to be effective listeners, it's crucial to be patient and consistent in your approach. Learning this talent takes time, particularly for young children.

Here are some tactics you might try to help your kid become a better listener consider Timing.

Parents typically want to discuss and be listened to promptly when they bring up a problem.

But it might be good to make sure that you are picking a moment when the kids is ready to listen.

Right in the midst of a game or during another chat may not be as beneficial as a little bit later.

Try something like, "I can tell you are busy right now; would there be a gap in a few minutes when we can talk?"

Doing so demonstrates you respect your child's time, something they may imitate in their own life after repeatedly seeing it in you.

One thing you may do when the kids are distracted during a discussion is to ask them to repeat what was said so that you know that the message was understood.

Repeating back is part of a method called active listening where a person's message is valuable enough to be reinforced by repetition.

Educating your kid on this core ability is the first step in teaching them to be effective listeners at home, with others, and at school. So, when you do have your conversation moment, ask them to tell you what they heard, Telling you back to you will also make the message simpler for younger children to recall.

Try not to criticize them if they struggle, but calmly repeat what was stated. Eventually, this talent will become second nature to them.

Parents should exercise active listening to help promote these abilities in their children.

1. Offer a Choice

When giving your kid a direction or asking them to do something, one useful strategy is to offer them an option.
Doing so empowers kids and helps them feel like they have some influence over their lives. Additionally, giving children an option builds strong decision-making abilities.

No longer are they simply following directions, but they are engaging in the things that touch their lives.

For instance, instead of saying "put on your dress, ask them whether they want to wear the red pajamas or the blue pajamas. Anytime you can offer your child an option, you should.

Then, when it's time for the instructions, when there is just one choice, people will be more inclined to listen.

2. Try Gentle Physical Touch

Bringing a child into a room to talk with them can be enhanced if you place your hand on their arm, wrap an arm around them, or gently squeeze their shoulders.
Children tend to learn in different ways, and when you use both verbal messages and appropriate touch, you can get their attention a little better.
Physical touch that is not as gentle can be a real problem when trying to communicate.

Make sure that your touching strategy is gentle, well-gentled, well-thought-out, and communicates love and respect.

3. Be Consistent

Kids learn best when the messages they receive are consistent. So make sure your expectations regarding listening behavior are clearly and consistently communicated. Your child should know what is expected and be working toward becoming a more active listener.

While it's important to be patient, you don't want to give your child mixed signals about the importance of listening.

By consistently interacting with them and communicating your expectations, you will eventually begin to see positive changes in their listening skills.

4. Rewards for Effective Listening.

Be creative about reinforcing your child's listening skills when they get it right. Praise your child when they display good listening skills or use small rewards in order to encourage good listening.

How to Use Rewards That Don't Cost Anything

First, you show people respect when you make time to listen to their problems, and it's simpler for them to show respect back when they feel appreciated.

Second, children learn much more from what they see than from what they hear, so make sure you're modeling the behavior you wish to see.

They will emulate your listening practices as they learn more about interpersonal interactions.
Take the time to chat when they are ready, and they will be more likely to react to you when you need them to listen.

How to Get Kids to (REALLY) Listen:

However, if you want to get a grasp on your child's unresponsiveness, the first thing you need to do is find out WHY he is not listening.

More often than not, his lack of responsiveness is a symptom, not the underlying issue. If you don't treat this problem at its roots, you're bound to see a simple instance of "not listening" blossom into major behavior concerns such as tantrums, stubbornness, and backtalk.

Why Don't Kids Listen?

Before we go any further, make sure you've checked out any probable medical issues that might be hurting your child's hearing or understanding. If you are convinced your child's ears are fully functioning.

Children of all ages have a hard-wired hunger for power because children DO have influence over their body and voice, the most frequent (and irritating) power battles occur when children use their bodies and words to resist adult wishes, by choosing NOT to listen, kids may demonstrate their authority.

This conduct is merely a way kids demonstrate their demand for greater control and decision-making power in their lives.

I'm not advocating you let them call every shot. By doing this, cooperation from your children will improve and the awful repeat – remind – repeat – remind cycle will come to an end.

When talking to parents, "not listening" frequently ends up being a blanket word that encompasses a plethora of concerns.

Because "not listening" is so broad, it might be difficult to identify a remedy.

I'm not suggesting there aren't instances when your kid is simply flat-out ignoring you—that happens!

However, more often than not, it's less about "not listening" and more about some underlying problem.

Is she weary, hungry, or not feeling well? Is there some underlying control issue causing her to disengage such as, Chores, Homework, Bedtime, Sibling frustrations?

Don't group every communication failure under the "not listening" umbrella.

Dig in and find out what's truly going on. Then you can build an action plan to directly address that issue on the following

1. Get on Their Level

When you need your child's attention, be sure you get her focus—that involves eye contact, when you lower yourself down and look her in the eye, you not only verify that she sees and hears you, but you deepen the connection as well.

This means you may have to move away from the washing or put down the whisk for a minute and go into the other room.

Proximity is key, you're not talking down to her or yelling commands from the other room–you're conversing with her. What did she want me to do instead?

That's unclear and conflicting, for example, if you say, "Don't touch your brother," a kids needs to cease the present action and choose the acceptable substitute behavior—if I can't touch him, does that imply I can't embrace him? Can I give him a high five?, Can I assist him with putting on his jacket or tying his shoes if mom asks? Instead, tell your child what to DO.

Instead of saying "Don't touch your brother," try "Use gentle touches when touching your brother" or "Your brother doesn't want to be touched right now, so please keep your hands folded while we are in the car."

2. Cut your speech in half.

I was as guilty of this as anybody parents, and particularly women, tend to convert a five-second response into a five-minute dissertation!

When attempting to capture your kid's attention, be as succinct as possible, and they won't even have time to tune you out!

3. Express Your Appreciation in Advance

Help your kids make an acceptable decision by taking this leap of faith, Your anticipatory "Thank you for hanging up your towel after your shower" will motivate your children far more than "I better not see your towel on the floor again!"

For instance, if you want your kid to stop watching television and join you at the dinner table, you can allow them to enjoy another 15 minutes of TV after dinner or before sleep provided they come right away without grumbling.

Offering a simple reward or incentive may assist in improving their listening habits.

Letting them know, in advance, that you trust them to do the right thing helps encourage open communication channels and boosts the possibility that the assignment will be finished.

Chapter 5

Tips to assist your kids communicate about their feelings & Developing Trust in them

Despite conventional belief, emotionally astute kids are not immune to spells of worry, fury, and other unpleasant emotions. And when those sentiments hit, they may do so with such ferocity that you and they both feel baffled and helpless.

I know this from experience, my spouse and I usually joke that our daughter was born anxious. We recognized quite early on those settings that other adolescents thought "normal" were nerve-racking for her.

Almost every change was accompanied by clinginess, weeping, and periods of eczema.

We placed all of our expectations on emotion regulation after listening to specialists and "reading everything."
Numerous studies have associated behaviors such as tantrums, meltdowns, excessive anxiety, and even aggressive actions like hitting and biting, with a failure to manage emotions properly.
Knowing your child’s emotion-driven behavior is normal to help, but having the tools to help them cope with those feelings when they strike is even better.
Teaching kidss to understand and regulate their emotions involves providing them with vital life skills.

Why does fostering your child's emotional intelligence matter?

Research involving emotional intelligence has indicated that adolescents educated about emotions are better equipped to create ways to eliminate stressful inputs. For example, emotionally intelligent kids are more likely to identify when to walk away from difficult settings, or they can choose items to engage in to calm their concerned or furious feelings.

The current research shows that adolescents who are aware of their emotions and know how to express them in a socially acceptable manner perform better at school.

Increase your social connections, and are more inclined to assume that they are in control of what occurs to them.

They are less prone to develop behavioral difficulties.

They are also more likely to be school-ready and cheerful than kids unable to manage their emotions.

1. Teaching your toddler to detect emotions.

The first step in boosting your child's capacity to handle overwhelming emotions is to train her to distinguish diverse emotions.

But this does not entail training her to conceal sentiments, rather, it is about educating her that emotions are normal—they are all around us—and she can govern how she responds to them.

It is not until they are roughly age 10 that kids begin to be entirely mindful of their emotions.

That said, emotional intelligence tests have shown that your kids may be educated about emotions from as early as age three.

Making it a practice to put her feelings into words – "I can see you're sad," or "I know you're disappointed because you would have liked to continue watching your show" - goes a long way in educating her to discern distinct emotions and put her sentiments into words.

Things to keep in mind to boost your child's emotional intelligence.

1. Talk frequently but for short durations of time.

It is more useful to share feelings frequently but for short periods than to talk infrequently but for lengthy periods.

2. Picking the correct timing matters.

Do not attempt to speak to your child about emotions when he is in the throes of a breakdown or when you're weary or upset, It won't work.

The perfect opportunity to communicate to your kids about emotions is when you are both calm, relaxed, and attentive.

3. Relate emotional dialogues to your child.

It is excellent to talk about emotions with your children.

Relating such sentiments to particular difficulties hurting your kids is even better. For example, if you're reading a novel about wrath, you may ask her what would make her as mad as the character in the book.
You may also ask her if she has ever felt the same as that character and what she did.
If your kids has trouble expressing sentiments, you may also encourage her to speak about them by asking her how a friend would feel if the same incident occurred to him or her.

But as many parents who have had to cope with extremely emotional kids know, attempting to establish "what works" to alleviate anxiety or other intense emotions is a hard area.

The difficulty is, the relationship between "emotions" and "coping methods" is not always evident.

What works now may fail miserably tomorrow, and what your child picks to effectively soothe a given emotionally arousing experience may have virtually no effect in another environment.

The good news is that there are several options your kids may pick from.

The "Emotions Kit" is a terrific resource loaded with different age-appropriate items (cards, games, worksheets, tools, etc.) and is meant to help you communicate with your kid about emotions.

It also includes numerous coping tactics your child may test.

How to talk with your kids about emotions.

While managing your child's strong emotions may be nerve-racking, it helps to remember that anxiety and anger are among the most regular and repeated feelings children suffer with, frequently well into puberty.
Also, it helps to know that most instances of emotional behavior in children are normal, and here is how to judge if your child's conduct should quit giving you sleepless nights:

1. Offer aid

The most essential thing you can do to assist ease your child's worry or anger is to speak about the problem.
Listening to your kids and asking questions that make her speak about the situation helps him understand the scenario from an objective perspective.
Questions such as "What are you most terrified of?" could offer you a framework on which to construct your assistance.

2. Don’t invalidate his feelings.

None of your child’s problems are too tiny to overlook. He needs to know that it’s alright to worry, or to be sad, or to be enraged and that everyone feels such feelings periodically.

Talk about the incidents that make you concerned or irritated and tell him how you manage your feelings.

Let your kids know that emotions are natural but that they can be addressed.

Teach her how to deal with powerful emotions.

Telling your kid "it's going to be alright" will not comfort her intense feelings.

What she needs are skills she can progressively employ by herself to cope with stressful conditions, the more routinely she adopts particular routines, the more those actions will become everyday habits.

The thing with kids is that while they may associate certain emotions (for example, anxiety before their swimming class) with certain coping mechanisms (for example, drawing), they will not necessarily associate a new anxiety-provoking situation.

Some kids can do so, but the majority are not.

This suggests that, in many situations, your baby will have to create new coping methods to cope with new conditions.

The Emotions Kit provides numerous coping mechanisms your kids could take in different settings to influence kids' emotional intelligence.

When is it time to seek assistance with your child's emotion-driven behavior?

Unfortunately, emotion-driven behavior in adolescents could suggest more major challenges needing the care of an expert.

Developing Trust and Belief in Your kids.

The capacity to trust oneself and others are at the core of every meaningful connection, and you may begin to establish your child's feeling of trust as early as infancy by being sensitive to her physical and emotional needs.

Studies have shown that when kids are comforted, it boosts their capacity to deal with stress and control their emotions.
As your kids matures, you may enhance her capacity to trust by providing a supportive culture where you listen and follow through on the commitments you make.

Show your kids that you trust them

Trust in relationships goes both ways, and by observing and empathizing with your kid, you are indicating that no matter what he/she does, you will always be there.

This translates into giving your kid somewhat more responsibility to see whether they can manage it or not.

Don't constantly anticipate success, and try not to react too forcefully if he or she accidentally smashes a glass.

Building abilities is a learning process, but by extending the choice, you are teaching your kid that you trust her.

You may feel upset with her, but always let her know that you have total faith in her abilities to make good judgments in the future.

Respect your child's demand for privacy. Trust also implies that you respect your child's right to keep certain topics private (unless in circumstances when it is essential to interfere).

Sometimes your kid may not want to speak about everything, and you need to respect that.

Your kids may not want to speak about school one day, or what she did during a play date, Unless you have cause to suspect that there is anything that needs to be discussed, it is acceptable to allow your child to have a portion of her life that is apart from you.

It is crucial at this stage of development that a kids has a nice sensation of independence from you while she establishes her self.

Playing with your kids or reading to her also helps establish a sense of trust.
Act out events with her fuzzy buddies, like having mother bear pick up baby bear from school or feeding baby bear when she's hungry.
These are wonderful strategies to educate your kids about ways you display your trust in regular settings.

Answering any questions she may have while you are playing will assure her that you have the competence necessary to take care of her, giving her greater faith in you.

This is also a good chance for your kids to learn about the role that trust plays inappropriate relationships and to remember to be careful around strangers and not soon trust everybody that she does.

www.ingramcontent.com/pod-product-compliance
Lightning Source LLC
LaVergne TN
LVHW050340160826
845677LV00014B/3702

* 9 7 9 8 3 5 7 6 0 0 1 9 6 *